More Praise for

Why I Am Like Tequila is one of the .... books to come out in years. Mendez takes us on a wild ride from birth, to family, to community, with a master's control of language and with gritos that sing and yawp and cry from the rooftops of the Americas. Unpredictable, imaginative, necessary, these poems introduce us to an important new poet for our generation.

—**Daniel Chacón**, author of *Hotel Juarez*

In this shining debut, Lupe Mendez writes the sometimes anguished, always rousing, ever defiant love songs of fatherhood. The son-as-father, carrying his old man out of the truck, the sting of his fist still on the son's jaw, the father-to-be, grieving a child that could not arrive. The teacher-father, sheltering with raging and tender heart the student whose own father faces deportation. These poems are storm and elegy, poems of sea foam, maguey, and moonlight. These are poems that ask: "Can you think of a lie you can tell me?" and poems that offer: "Let me shout your name."

—**Lena Khalaf Tuffaha**, author of *Water & Salt*

In poems as intimate and outward as they are formally bold in disposition and address, Lupe Mendez connects the murderous brutality of events in Mexico and Latin America to scenes of U.S. violence involving citizens of color and immigrants caught in the institutional racism of church and state and law enforcement. "I am every grave / found in / Juarez, Sayula, Ayotzinapa… Caracas, Jasper, Sugar Land/ the next space, a next space, that next space." The poet's recognition of childhood hardship links his simultaneous life as artist, teacher, son, husband, and father to working class family histories in the precarious US American economy; to vigilante justice and terrorism on the borderlands; to the joyful sensation of blasting cumbias, quarreling lovers, park lights, and kinships, in a tribute to places like Magnolia Homes or in honor of the undocumented to whom Hurricane Harvey recovery efforts are indebted. Moving seamlessly between English and Spanish, Lupe Mendez re-enchants the world in poems that take root in the intensity and exaltation that accompany breathing—"el sonido de alas / un millón de alas en el viento."

—**Roberto Tejada**, author of *Full Foreground*

WHY I AM LIKE TEQUILA

Poems

LUPE MENDEZ

WILLOW BOOKS

Detroit, Michigan

Why I Am Like Tequila: Poems

Copyright © 2019 by Lupe Mendez

Editor: Randall Horton
Cover art: Ramiro Rodriguez, www.RamiroRodriguez.com

ISBN 978-1-7322091-7-6
LCCN 2019939906

Willow Books, a Division of Aquarius Press
www.WillowLit.net

Printed in the United States of America

Acknowledgments

The following poems in this collection have appeared in the listed journals, anthologies or literary magazines in one form or another:

"In Honor of Magnolia Homes", *Bayou Review*, Vol. 1, Issue 50 – Fall 2012

"So How Are You Feeling Today?", *Luna Luna Literary Journal* – Fall 2014

"Flight", *Luna Luna Literary Journal* – Winter 2014

"When A Student Dies", *Ostrich Review* – Summer 2015

"A Human Rights Worker Tells Me About the Cuarenta y tres", *The Thing Itself* – Spring 2015

"A Dancer Tells Me About the Cuarenta y tres", *HeART Journal Online* – Fall 2015

"Layers", *The New Sound: A Journal of Interdisciplinary Art & Literature* – Fall 2015

"The Reason We Don't Come Over For Your Daughter's Birthday", *BorderSenses* – Vol. 12, Fall 2015

"The Exorcist on TV the Night Hurricane Alicia Fell" *Pilgrimage* –Winter 2016

"Photograph of 'Woman on Street - Flower Leis'", *Gulf Coast Literary Journal* – Spring 2016

"Why I am Like Tequila" *Gigantic Sequins Literary Journal*, Issue 2, Volume 7 – Summer 2016

"Photograph of 'Woman in Red Dress, Sunflowers, Sitting With Blanket'", *Imaniman/ Split This Rock Anthology* – Fall 2016

"Photograph of 'Woman on Street – Blue Scarf, Red Dress'" – *Literal Literary Journal* – Winter 2017

"To the Priest Who Told One of My Students That Holding a Forum on Campus Could Make the Kids Act Like 'the Savage Latinos' He Saw on TV Burning Trump Piñatas", *Texas Review,* Summer 2017

"Un soñador al momento que le dicen que no", *Texas Review* – Summer 2017

"Prayer of a Workhorse", *Glass: A Journal of Poetry* – Fall 2017

Advice on My First Night in the Kitchen at the Garden Restaurant", *A Dozen Nothing* – Summer 2018

"Angustia vs. Silence, *A Dozen Nothing* – Summer 2018
"Manos (or Prayer Holding Night)", *A Dozen Nothing* – Summer 2018

"Mercy", *A Dozen Nothing* – Summer 2018

Contents

Part IV—Maguey [Body]

"quiero morirme como muere mi pueblo"
—José Alfredo Jiménez (¡Presente!)

"We make the world better"
—Anthony "Zin" Mills (¡Presente!)

Why I Am Like Tequila

Part I—Raices [Roots]

Layers

I. Lupillo

I asked apa why this name.
He laughed. *The night you were*
born, your ama almost died,
toxemia in veins, and outside,
the moon was a breeze. He asked

about ama in broken English.
The doctor told my father,
pray – only one will make it.
Tio Chilo once said apa sharpened
glass pieces to shave. I asked,

how did apa not cut himself?
Tio laughed, *muchacho, cada*
hombre se corta. blood is nothing.
Ama said on my born day, she
floated out of body in a red line.

Saw herself, heard a baby coo.
Ama had to have a hysterectomy.
Perhaps age or I broke womb.
The night my apa first crossed Tejas,
he prayed la virgencita would guide

him. He prayed to a breeze, a moon.
I imagine him in prayer the night
I was born, in a capilla. *Querida*
Virgen dejamelos vivos. My body,
my ama's blood pooled in this name.

I've wondered if I am the bestia
he asked for. I have not fought,
howled at the moon like he. I haven't
mixed mud, sweat, the way ama has.
But, I've been lumbre every night.

II. La Negra, La India (La Virgen de Extremadura)

the first man she meets is a doctor/Lucas/dresses her in reds and golds/ says he likes black girls/puts her on a pedestal/asks if she wants to leave Syria/they travel red dirt roads/where the mirasol grows/they come across the caballero Gil/she asks him to build a templo for her/he does/he dies in the last brick/between the mortar and the fingers there's a rumor/an Italian with three boats/he wants to sail to some new place/asks her to come along/they sail awhile/she watches the skies/he eats all the granadas the night before landing/yells he plans on staying/the new neighbors don't understand/they mumble between themselves/they bring food/fancy pots/ mounds of gold/he answers them/in cut off limbs/in dog chase bites/in ankle shackles/separating babies/small pox/mixed up tongues/dead horses

she goes up in the hills/walks a while/meets a poor boy/Juan/asks him to build her a place to stay/says he knows a guy/who knows a guy/who knew the lady that lives here/up the block in Tepeyac/lady eats maize raw/lets the kernels stick to her teeth/talks to deer/has a house of mud/it was burnt down/still hangs around in the trees/in the mouths of the dying/in the ears of corn

they meet/trade some stars/they embrace/they kiss and stay together/she gives Juan some roses for his troubles/all the neighbors/they come by/bring candle/bow their heads/raise arms to the sky/sometimes/one of them goes out on the porch/watch as they all talk at once/how they cut the necks of goats/paint the doorways with blood/they ask her to bless some crops or watch over them/like she was going to make flowers appear/like in the snow or something

III. December 12th

My bones lay in,
        a river,
        a howl at all the blood moons,
               the lights,
               the candles

       in front of an altar, not far away.
                           I am in the womb in
Tonanzin,
          mother of earth,
          her son her little
          adobe sun, who hides ideas
        in stones, washes them
        in paints,

        paints in lyrics,
          in newsprint, draws Catrinas,

                   in pastles, the color of lasers
                   in la oscuridad, the color of poverty,
                   charcoal and rib cages showing
hueso blanco,
        waiting to be put to rest.

Soy llanto.
Soy virgin,
        un degraciado santo,
                   a mountain chained to the wind,
                   a paper treaty, betrayed, moaned, abandoned.

Soy

                   Jose Guadalupe Posada, hungry,
                   Guadalupe Victoria, victorious,
                   Jose Guadalupe Olivares, aka, a
poetry god.

I am La Unión del Pueblo Entero. Punto.

I am

a canine,
a Puertorican songstress,
a Mexican Banda barbaro,
a kick-pusher.

I live   in black volcanic rock
burning, streaming against river,

against the wolves en lo hondo del rio,
in the bottom of the water,

where you can dream in colored light,
dream, dream, dream.
Dream of me.

Part II—Mezontle [Heart]

The Leftovers of Mermaids

My mother would tell me
to jump over the waves
at the beach. The foams,

are the leftovers of mermaids.
Do not step on them. Admire
the sea, let it embrace you

in salty brown gulf waters.
Dip your cuts, your ulcers,
under waves. Wash away oil

spots in water. Cover up sins,
eat away time in wind and rays.
Inhale summer days that sift in

restless sand, covering sneaky
promiscuous hands.

My mother never mentioned

ulcers, sins, restlessness –

Just jump over the waves.
I always imagine the rest

each time a cop would catch
me on the beach with my girl,
on our East Beach,

uncovering nakedness and sin.
This sea. Perfect, sweet, sin.

First Memory in 180 Syllables

A three year old, black hair, dips forward on
a staircase, fingers a Miller High Life,
it falls. His eyes roll back a flip, bottle flicks
hollow, down yellow stairs, gold spiraling,
this splinters against a block concrete step,
wet silence breezes with a blink. A father
breaks out the door, he swings at boy, shoves
boy tumbles forward, arms, feet, all limbs slap
wooden edges, this father watches a
little frame roll a crumbling way, a
brown body toward broke shards. The boy is
scooped up at the twenty-third step, his uncle
stares at father, a shot up the stairs, body
is dazed, the focus on the body is
a slow shoot on the scrapes – the bloody nose,
the cut along the cartilage, raise eyes,
this broken body, that broken glass both
on the last concrete step drip slick copper.

Rod Stewart, Six Inches from the Wall

In the afternoon, Rod Stewart plays on the T.V.
Cathode rays cover muscles, flexing naked in
colors brighter than dark skins pulsating
to the music. Sweet sweat speaks a rhythm

in bed. Inside sheets, the babysitter and her
novio pause. They entrench gritos, brown lips.

a moment:

Shhh – I'm trying to hear
the blond man sing.

A five year old sits and shares the room
at the base of the bed atop their clothes.

He taps his feet, eats the images, the mic,
the raspy voice, the base guitar,
the saxophone, the panties, the bra,
the rubber's wrapper, a pack of menthols.
He listens to her caderas curving, novio's
pecho broad, the clinched hands, biting skin
until he can no longer
take the groans and the besos.

He walks away from the T.V. set, six inches
from the wall, so the vecinos don't complain
about the noise. He leaves it on. He leaves
his babysitter's legs in the air, wrestling.
He opens the door, sees a little girl outside.
baila un paso- like Rod, crotch ready, bouncing,

smiling on beat. He sings quietly on his way out –
come on sugah, let me know.

Driving by the Old State Theater on Ama's 79th Birthday

She damn near snaps her neck,
eyes stick to the fachada,
an old movie house, bare,
gutted white inside. She smiles,
looks, says,

I know why
you such a bruto, mi'jo.

Unfolds an old memory,
back in Fifty-Eight,
downtown Galveston has signs,
big, stark white black letter signs
Colored here, Colored
there, nothing

para invisible Mexicanos.

Unknown, unless
you make a mistake—
dangle you in a tree branch
late at night. Rent lady tells me
to be careful at night. Used to
babysit Anita and her pigtails,

a nursing school hustle, a barter.
Anita had a friend,
                        Ama goes on,
beautiful, plump, black, small
Olivia.

Ama loved to teach the girls
how to cook on Saturdays,
pancakes, eggs, eat warm syrup
with a spoon, buy them dolls,
watch them struggle

with time tables and takes them
to the movie house. In front,

it had signs, big, stark white black
letter signs, No Colored
here. *In the building,*

mi'jo, I am bruta, then. Now.

I love Galveston Island winters,
a reason to hide the girls
in my pea coat.
Pay the janitor.
Sneak them through the back door,
their hands warm—sticky
from sweet maple. Their heads

unaware of hate. Their eyes,
their skins are the same in the dark.

Cada Mañana in San Benito, TX

"And I know a spot right over the hill"
—Hank Williams Sr., 1951

Tia Maria's shotgun house hides in
between years of cherry blossom limbs,
        in buck shots of leaves that settle on the roof,

on the stepping stones, on the porch, flakes
along the grass. I am here to collect summer
        aguacates, the fresh cheeks of strawberries

and consejos, the size of dollar bills. I come here
every summer, to the hot house, to the white
        tiny leaves that blind me to old poverty,

to the locust winds outside, to the smell
brewing Sanka and canela.
        I come here to finesse my 13 year old words

against the ears of Olivia, or Emelda, Carmen
or Monica. One of them will take a walk with me.
        Remind me to walk under the blossoms at night.

The stars are much larger to talk about
and under the blossoms, nothing else matters.
        I live in the past, watching my mother fighting

in the streets, a challenge of who can fit the most
fresas in their mouth. A strawberry runs down a smile.
        I sleep on a bed frame, a family tree now, a witness

to each birth in this family. Everyone sleeps here
when they are young. The radios play tunes
        older than me. Every morning a shot rings out.

I can hear my Tia belting a song. Her voice blasts
on the porch swing; an alarm that will echo in me,
        a high pitch for the rest of my life,

a nasal cry—a fuzzy radiola memory stirs.

Hey good looking, wha'tcha got cookin?
How's about cooking something up with me?

The Exorcist **on TV the Night Hurricane Alicia Fell**

Due to the severe damage, the name "Alicia" was retired
in the spring of 1984 by the World Meteorological Organization,
and will never be used again for an Atlantic hurricane –
it was replaced with "Allison" for the 1989 season.
Coincidentally, in 2001 the name "Allison" was retired
after striking the same area as Alicia.
—*National Hurricane Center, 2010*

My family split up that day, my mother, white scrubs, dressed
for her sick-people-in-the-head job, my father, quiet, - watched
black clouds, white flash cracks. The sun hadn't offered a thing.

I couldn't understand the swirls on the screen, the buzz, the ripples,
the arrows that pointed across the TV. , but I felt the swoon,
the house swayed with the wind. I smelled sea salt. It made me jerk,

mess up my horse picture, brown, and black with yellow hair.
I heard the seagulls, they laughed as they flew away. I drew them, too,
saw them as they joined the rest of the people in cars and their lights,

those that ran from the water. I told my father I worried
about mother, said she would be home that night. He kept working
in between swigs of Miller High Life and duct tape. I helped him

in the afternoon, x all the windows, between trips to the bar next door.
I prayed for food. I did not eat that day. In the distance, the breaks
in the waves grew tall, throwing up jetty rocks on the roadway, crushed

a man, covered him in granite and sea foam. He didn't even make a grip
when he died. His hand was limp, his wrist was stuck between asphalt,
the glistening rock, the size of the Datsun he was walking toward.

The smell of fish remained when they pried the piece of jetty off – he died
with a basket full of croakers. He once shined shoes at the Hotel Galvez,
he knew everyone and told my father tales about old hurricanes

being brutal lovers and about bitter women who found him out in a cheat.

He sat by the waves a lot, taught me how to make paper boats
float in the waves and taught me how to fly kites in storms.

On the TV that night, I watched a white girl who's head spun
around, who spoke in a demon voice, who beat on her mother, threw
a dresser at her, who made the flower filled walls of her house shake,

who made the red stop sign from the corner of the block fly through
our window, made the wind howl with gnarling rain, who made the door
splinter right next to me. The TV blinked black, flung against the wall,

not a picture moved, but I still heard her laugh, a bit of maple wood in my arm.
The door was gone and out of its space, the lights of the town emptied.
Only the black, only the lanterns and the twigs, the bushes and the sand,

the colored cars and telephone wires circled overhead, floating in the breeze.

What My Father Really Means

I

Si trabajas dos jales y andas de prisa – nomas échate agua caliente en el pelo, los sobacos y enjuaga tu perico y caracoles.
[The days will grow into each other, the work hours addict you, the mind falls asleep in upright double shifts, there is nothing wrong with work, with washing your dick in the sink, means you can't miss a minute making money. Clean yourself. Wipe away the tired in hot rags then go back to hustle y trabájale]

II

Al manejar un carro – tu nomas písale mijo, el que se pone encima, atropella el hijo de su rechingada madre.
[You will hear these words said to you: mojado, spic, pocho, americano, wetback, beaner, marijuano, brownie, darkie, alien, illegal, boy, dirty, greaser, roach, rat, flea, anchor baby. Ignore the air they float on. Tilt your head toward the yellow of the sun, darker. Grow warmer. Build laugh. Dig dance move into the space between these words, these voices, so the only sound heard is a gruñido in their stomachs.]

III

No busques bronca, pero si aparece, mételes un putazo.
[I will be the one to teach you how to fight. You will need to defend yourself from people who disrespect you. I'll pelt fists against your frame. This will be the first memory I place in you: you will drop a miller high life from my hands and I will hit your temple, watch you roll down a flight of wooden stairs. You will know the taste of varnished wood lodged in your gums. Smile. We will do this often. Come here and let's begin.]

IV

Méate la mano si te cortas bien mal, luego échate tierra, al rato, tendrás callos bien hechos.
[Take care of your hands. You will wash windows and plates and avoid glass in streets. You will remember playing a las escondidas at night, the slice from broken glass as you fall, your hand slick red, palm up – remember the feel of a hot stream from you to wash away a trickle of blood. You will feel the same sting the day you first clean windows. You will have just popped blisters on your palms, submerge your hands into a pail to reach for rags, rush back to that night, piss coating your hand, the sting, the strong smell

30

of ammonia will never leave your nostrils. But your skin will be thicker and those windows will glisten, not a crack among them.]

V
Si se te para ese chilio en los pantalones, guárdalo para tu novia.
[You will find a young girl your age, care for her, you will laugh as you grope and flash body parts, you will flush in the face, blow blood vessels on beach nights, the smell of coconut scented sunblock coating your girl, and you will not have to go to her, with money in your hand, to a room above a bar, a nervous wreck, an exchange of service, an empty physical drive, to fuck with barely a word spoken, the sound of a radiola below her bed, the light scent of sweat and her skin cold, you will never have to know el barrio rojo mijo, because you will know how to talk to women in ways I didn't know they should have been spoken to.]

A Boy with Twisted Wrist

I wanted to spend too much time with her, alone,
along the beach – whisper a bit longer under moonlight

ripples. I should have worked a little bit harder
in the front cab of the truck, steam things up between

us, the windows with palm prints and lips.
Instead, I got home early, walked in the front door,

the throb of blood still bulging in my pants. I tasted
a morsel, perfume on my tongue, senses reacted to

the sound of my heart in my head, the smell,
"Japanese Cherry Blossom" on my hands. I was slow.

I swallowed beer-drenched knuckles that came out
the doorframe. My father guarded the insides

from the outsides with a murmur, a stumble. I got up,
blood cut copper along my jaw, face pulsed along the lips,

slowly formed my mouth, swirled a few words:
I'm home. I took her home. I brought the truck back.

I walked him in, like a thousand times before, like rolling
a life size rock, damp with liquor, up the stairs, every night,

him, off to bed, a jumble of uneven buttons, a beer gut
and blood shot laughter that rose in mangled

arms and stumbled knee caps. I bore his weight
until I couldn't hold all that tension, couldn't see

in the dark of his eyes. I tried to catch a glimpse of affection.
But all I managed was a blow to my head, again, one.

I felt it all coming down on me, his weight, a split second,
my hand between her hips, twisted wrist, cupped her breasts

in my hands, and then they burned. I cupped her image,
sliced away, cupped the end of a machete, a slice in my palm,

a machete in the dark that sat against the corner of the hall;
in the corner of a moment, in the dark of the truck,

in the hallway. I searched for light, but all I could see
was how much I missed him in the daylight. I missed my girl

that moment. My hand knew the taste of steel, knew the taste
of warm thighs on fingertips, my lips wanted to bite into flesh.

I wanted to let loose, but I settled down. I struggled with
this unconscious liquor, I rested there, at my father's feet,

at the bottom of the stairs again, my one hand, still holding
his neck, still bleeding in the other, there in the dark. Awake.

I wondered how they both slept, how they dreamed hot, how
much I wanted them in the bosom of promiscuous night.

Advice On My First Night in the Kitchen at the Garden Restaurant

I see you   in between the blurs of sous-chefs,
in bits of ladles that stick out of soups.

Careful,

         don't let your sleeves get caught   in chicken
stock flows around   stove tops   or the prep cooks,

skimming around that metal table, brilliant.

You should hustle here   a few days more.   Nights
stay with you,   with the hot rags   in water,

waves of dishes steaming,   your fingers stinging
         from cold and hot   and flushed and chilled red
steaks, raw

under the blade.   White tendons
nerve out on tan boards.   We all get past

the fumbling flops of food   on floor.   You can pinch
         black headed strawberries,

                    sink chocolate warheads,
settle them on mirrors,   eat each shard, you can

take one.   See? We always take two.
         Go ahead,
learn to make extra,

                    shhh
                    eat a brown pepper steak,

in butter rolls.   It's the best meal in eight hours
standing,   planning your escape,

pulling
         green lettuce into sheets,   count the clock ticks,

34

multiply that

by the four dollars,   twenty-five cents we make.
                     Go crazy broke.

When you cut yourself, flesh   in the palm,

     that becomes
           the only long break
     rummage around the back

ask everyone you haven't met for the first aid kit.

     Go again, in between short order cook arms
     in sauces and pesto
coated vegetables.
               Don't touch the radio.
It's one hour Tejano,
        one hour Norteño,
           two hours Magic 102 Jams.

That's the secret to peace.
           You still bleeding a bit?
     Get yourself an old rag,
        a black rag.
Let go of the knife.
     Let's dip your hand   in the ice machine.
               Stain the ice melts,

        eat that with me,
   the taste, the copper pennies,   the nickels,
        the dimes,
        they pay us to work
           until the lights go out.

Manos (or Prayer Holding Night)

a fist no
bullets out
the pop of skin
the twist of wrist
where scars pox out
coals rubbed together
where the air runs to hide
first seconds of fresh wound
el significado de un trancazo
gutting a confetti of fish scales
tocando Dos Monedas siempre
the rash that spiders into bleed
reaching out in a pitch so black
gripping collected corn stocks
looking for change in pockets
metal across jawbones biting
bricks against me, against me
combs of warm water in hair
bandages holding paychecks
shovels up in the wet ground
translators when tongue slurs
a shave with a sizzling knife
abriendo ataud sin pésame
age measured in caguamas
red slices to a calf's throat
the nails that scratch white
dotted knuckles magnetic
cold bones on card tables
blisters wrapped in mint
a heart that waits to beat
a shake in the forearms
glass shards in tendons
boxing practice lessons
seconds jabbing reflex
boiled water thrown
thunder up on body
hacksaw for limbs
weighted fingers
axes split roots
the snap of ribs
a flung machete
palms cup clap
tenderness waiting
prayer holding night

36

In Honor of Magnolia Homes

In Honor of Mr. Michelleti and his jacked up eye, who could never point to the right price on the back wall of the meat market and ring you up for the ham you desperately needed to make a sandwich on a Sunday,

In Honor of Doña Maria, with her arthritic knuckles that were cold to the touch; she would actually say she loved the green make- up on the wicked witch of the west – both *cabronas* scared the hell out of my 7 year old ass,

In Honor of *El Novio*, the self proclaimed ladies man, who would take me by the hand and walk up and down the beach yelling out that "we should play, Frisbee, *mijito*" in front of the young girls he wanted to talk to,

In Honor of all the neighborhood public schools that thought I was mentally retarded and didn't click to the idea that I only spoke a bold Spanish and lost me to an all *negrito* Southern Baptists school that labeled everything in the building so I could finally learn to say *tank jews* out of gratitude,

In Honor of Mr. Streater and his bigoted voice as he constantly yelled from his window for us to turn down the *Vicente Fernandez*, because he couldn't drink his Schlitz in peace,

In Honor of Marcus, with his sling shots and bruising rocks that managed to get us a slick switch to our *nalguitas* from everyone in the neighborhood, until someone hit him with a bullet in his lung.

In Honor of Fr. Frank and his funny accent in Spanish, it just provided him with a new congregation that didn't care about the rumors of him and little white girls,

In honor of Carmona, who used to buy us orange, sticky, push- up pops with money from her push-up bra that she wore when she ran the corners from 6pm to mid-night,

In Honor of Gladys, the bus driver who always gave me a free lift to the library, daily, after a fight in the street,

In honor of my mother who worked too hard and still had time to tell me a story, and yet I could never tell her mine,

37

In honor of my Tio Reymundo who showed me how to treat a lady – *like a dog, mijito,* he real lonely now.

In honor of Lulu, the girl I wanted, who I told too late, who moved to El Chuco,

In honor of my Father, and his abundance of Miller Lite,

In honor of getting left outside when he's had too much to drink,
In honor of the gun shots in my walls and connect the dot games,

In honor of Streater's Tavern with its fight nights,

In honor of the spot where I think Marcus died,

In honor of old orange brick,

In honor of blanquitos and blacks,

In honor of eight tracks,

In honor of the Platters,

In honor of Los Bukis,

In honor of duct tape windows,

In honor of rumors –
Like the one I heard about Marcus' last words,

> *get my mom, she'll know what to do.*

In honor of his mom.

Lagrimas de Mi Barrio

I play around orange dirt outside the house, a small open lot a mound   the grain of it gets under my nails
grits itself   along my back   I trek it   get English lessons daily
from the mouth of a girl blond green little eyes   teaches me play sky daddy bar angry secret hide seek

We do this for weeks
It is the first time I have ever seen a white

                                              girl   First time I ever feel English in my ears

I cannot say her name   her father's name   Him at the bar next door   a blonde mustache
the girl and I play hide, seek for a bit that day;   until I lose her,   I run up and down the callejón
excuse me alley say alley   between the bar   my yellow house   she teaches me yellow teaches me house
teaches me shhhh   her father comes outside to find her
he comes

he screams at me – the alley I say   and he leaves   I know
she is not there   I look   the mound   climb and seek   catch the edge   her shoe in a bush   laugh –
you there – she comes out laughing her father behind grabs her   a talon around snake skinny arms pulls her away.

I hear him say something   I do not understand the something   I go
inside   speak to my mother   her washing the dishes   the sink   singing a tune   drops of Cornelio Reyna   I ask
Ana   ¿qué quiere decir wetback?

She stops washing   She looks up   in the air   a crack in the ceiling   she laughs   takes off her yellow gloves   she
kneels down on the ground   a tear fills one eye   it does not fall   cleans the dirt from my hands   says
mijito de mi vida   it is what they call   smart boys who   leave this desgraciado barrio

39

The Boys at the Tennis Courts

drink malt liquor and sit on park
tables. They crack a cold idea that
susses out the sides of their mouths –

Wait   *until the lights go out, homie,*
             climb that shit up the chain link.

Wait   *with empty bottles, güey,*
             aim them at the tennis courts.

The park, the courts, full of young
gente blasting cumbias, playing on
columpios, full of ladies and lords.

No one's ever played tennis there,
meditation room for quarreling lovers,
where ritual dance is arranged

for a quince, chalk X's y la señora
Anita who tells you where you need
to stand.

No one pans back to the three of them.
Bottles empty. No one notices them
sitting beneath an oak tree, a 7:30 pm

shade, the hustle of Wednesday evening,
the lights over the courts. They come
out of hiding, feel their way up the chain

link. A slow climb, a bottle or two,
stuffed in oversized khaki Dickies.
A slip of the foot, a pause to see

if anyone else notices. They move
up, easy. The park lights haven't turned
off yet. It's not 8:00 pm. They wait,

each straddle on the fence,
the oak branches hide them in leaves,
a sudden fear of falling and a whisper–

fuck it.

They throw glass grenades, hold
their eyes at blurs of bodies, watch
people run themselves, cut themselves

afraid. The boys, they freeze for minute,
they look around the ground
for survivors – not a body in sight, not

a sound, but a quick clank
of the floodlights. It is 8 pm
and they take in the silence, take in

the scent of Oleanders, flood lights hum,
these boys perch upon the castle walls.
These boys at the courts, they be kings.

Mexican Island

I live in forty-five granite rocks in long rows.
This is a pier, a walkway, a moment jettisons
out into the gulf, just past the beach.
The world changes

here. The moon takes care of me.
I am drawn—moonlight,
a brush of sea air,
foam against the jagged that makes this place.

I park one block away. It is always dark
when I walk the Seawall, down the staircase

on 35th St.
I sit just at the edge, where mist collects,
                                        where
bare skin turns sticky salt, where city lights die.

I face the Gulf, the storms, white flashes,
shadows in the grey. Me quito las chanclas
de perdido Stretch toes.
Sand spreads under a midnight foot.

I take a swig of thunder, cheap whiskey,
unos traguitos de mezcal. I have sat with sad eyes.
I will sit with sonrisas, I shall bring my media costilla

here. I confess to the stars. I imagine myself
some place else. I watch the night change, watch
the tides bruise and break so much, they swell up.

I picture me—thrust myself upon the color horizon.
Jump away into the sea. I will not be able to,
the current along the rocks will drown, rip me.

This is the act—wishing, the act of island, being
at home, longing to be mid air, to be caught
in one large wave—to disappear into some deep.

42

This is the where the island bends. This jetty, this is
the closest finger into the ocean. I live here. I live.
I hold myself against this want.

Search Party (A Poem For the Mother of Jessica Cain, Missing Since 8.17.97)

"They buried their dead with the flowers in the field
with wounds so deep they never be healed"
—Sanders Bohlke

I.
She was at the water's edge,
a touch of the moon lit up her hair.
She was the center of a hug, a laugh,
a story people loved to tell. When
she disappeared, the breeze shifted,
collected the night in silent scraps.
She was young. There was no struggle.
There was no fight, just her purse
in the car, the keys lost, parked along
an I-45 at the end of road. Rumors ran
red across the bayou – that Jessica
ran away with a black boy, who'd a
thought of that? Little lady took off with
the wrong crowd. All them drugs in the air,
all those theatre kids dreaming shit.
Yet, nothing really ever found - locked car,
between exits, the house just over there,
a quick road away. She was almost home.
People gathered, sang her songs,
interchanged weepy candles, and dug
into the ground, prayed she was hiding in
the brush, in the marsh, dirty, misled.
So they searched, dragged the rumors into
their dreams, called her soon-to-be-college,
said, she's a bit tied up right now,
wrapped caution tape to broken branches
and Ziploc-ed socks on the side as evidence.
No one saw her smile again. Everyone just
looked at pictures. Pointed out where the car
was, alone. Someone said " the mom still runs her
a bath," put her clothes out every night
for a year, took up all sorts of things, read
all the books in the house, again, learned
how to flip bay houses, restored the furniture.

Poor thing, those the only legs and arms and backs
she could manage. She stripped the grime,
wiped the dull off, afraid to move away, lingered
a while – listened for the sound of feet on humid
wood, up the stairs, down the hall, until the tears
ran her out, and her own age wouldn't stall.
The summer sailed in. No one could whisper
a word, could live in weight. Some just prayed,
their hands shook, and their children, watched
for a missing girl,
a moment every day,   along the shore.

II.
        On a Tuesday night,
I flip in my skin,   a tear thuds
outside me – your face on the news
again.   Nineteen years later,
your face, still as bright as   I remember.
An old man, dying man,
            a fidgeting man rustles his dry twig
legs around an abandoned barn –
he points for the cameras,   tells the cops
where he thinks   he left you.
        There, the cameras, the tickertape
    at the bottom of the screen slicks
the words out

"MAY HAVE NEW INFORMATION ON THE DISAPPERANCE OF ..."

– I don't even fucking listen
anymore. I click around my keyboard,
remembering   all the machete hacks
in the evening breeze,   clearing brush
on the outskirts of La Marque,   in tree lines
                                off of Interstate 45.
The days spent   looking for you
in the thickets around our home –   I moan.
        Memory moans. You are just out of reach.
You are thirty miles from us, then.

45

You are present in voice
when I tell   my high school students
to not let a moment   slip away.   I watch
the videos people put up of   you.
          I attend the service. I smile at faces.
I smile at your parents. I   see you mother –
          remember how someone   once told me
your mother would run a bath for you
          – run a wish, run tears forever for
your return. Return, now you have,

                              now you have.

Breathe us in, Jessica, linda,   forgive me
that I didn't know you better.   I have no place
                    but to write of you, to remember,
to spend words on your voice and   wish you
well. I picture you now,   resting, in a tub,
          relaxing in the steam of water,
in a white bathroom,   candles lighting
the everywhere,   a single drip from the faucet,
and you resting, as you should be. Rest.
                              It's been so long without you.

Why I Am Like Tequila

I have pencas[1]
growing out of my body,
beautiful blue   maguey veins
stretching,   brown hands. Breathe in
              the sun.

Let me bleed   slowly.
        Every seven years I am
birthed,   dissected, cannibalized.
When I am useless,   bury my husk
in black wreaths[2].   Que toquen
conjunto[3] next to white candles,
lit on nights when the moon won't
shine. Drink   for me.
        Cry for me.
Mi corazón es un mezontle[4],
layers in white flesh,
in the center,   white
blood cells,   nectar seeping

---

[1]Penca—(n) The arm of a maguey,   a leaf, a blade, an arm—
that stretches   out, that reaches out, that flexes out,
that fleshes forward, the first limb that touches   the dew, that extends
into a the palm of a mejicano.

[2]Black Wreathes—(una chingadera) mi apa won't let us put a wreath on the door,
says it's the blanquitos who want to   remember death. That is why you have
a wreath, a simple announcement—someone just died. The first time
my ama and him drove around in 1974,   he couldn't breathe—
asked why so many people died in the month of December.
        Shook his head, mas triste.
        Shook his head, said "me acuerdo del Señor Davila"
              died from a fever, ran around
              one summer,
durante el tiempo de las lluvias,   recogiendo sus caballos

[3]Conjunto—n. The name of a genre of Mexican, Chicanx, Tex-Mex, Cuban music, featuring
instruments including fingers, bajo sextos, hearts, vocal chords, harps, adobe, violines, agonia,
liquor, dirt floors, botines, acordiones, espíritu, gente huasteco, gente jarocho, pobreza, riqueza, a
dance hall, two back up singers making a dollar each in 1968, and a look out to make sure la jura or
the Texas rangers don't show up to string someone on the branch of a roble [an oak tree, baboso, an
oak tree].

through to my heart sack,
greso, ready to fight.
Cut this out,   fracaso y espinas—
boil it   in fire, bursting
out of its chambers,   warm,
viscous and clear across my chest.
It beats in the heat of the day.
Soy jimador[5]   con su talache[6],
who is alone   in uneven cerros,
who clears rocks   that clutter growth,
who won't leave   until the job is done,
who digs   in the night,
who's back is good   enough to plow,
who goes home and   fucks,
who is determined   to plant a good seed,
who eats with his hands,
who sleeps   in the callejones of magueys,
who dreams before   his heart is plucked,
who cuts at ladrones   in the fields
who cleans cazangas[7]   after a dirty battle.

---

[4]Mezontle—(a heart) the gritty center   in the center of the plant where
tequila comes from. Your soul emanates   from this grainy thing, fluid a bit, not blood,
but molten rock,   your soul comes from water,   comes from mercury, runs recio, runs hot,
why you love until you are cold,   wear a sweater
when you touch,   lock eyes, embrace for warmth,   feel in
the chest for this ember,   this ember,   this ember.

[5]Jimador—(n) every mejicanx who has ever lived, who has ever died, who has ever sweat, who sing
corridos, a trio, a bolero, a cumbia, the image of a huichol, a rascuachero, a G.I. Joe, a mariachi, a
viejo, una reina, una diosa, una tamalera, the man who makes the liquor you love to down in a sing
shot glass [you wasteful shit] by pulling up the root for your drink, by pulling up your job, by worki
when you spend time reading this poem and resting. Right now, he is at work. Call back later.

[6]Talache—(really, yo?) a tool, a pick axe, older than you, shares the age with dirt, with work, with
iron, with rust, with wood, with houses, with bridges, with dig, with dug, with ditch, with edge, wit
groove.

[7]Cazanga—(nombre) **uno.** A sickle, a tool, sharp, cuts into a half moon,   leaves in a half moon,
dos. The tool of revolution in September. **tres.** The primo-hermano to the machete and the talache
cuatro. The shit ninjas would use   if they were originally from Mejico/ Centro America.
cinco. The thing under my bed   to ward off evil spirits. **seis.** a weapon born at the same tim
as Huitzilopochtli, a slick of his copete—the moment he was born,   he took it, spat on it,
made it metal,   made it hot,   what he used it to cut at his sister, making her head the mo
and his brothers, making them the stars [that boy real good, ¿escuchaste? al puro cien].

48

Part III—Pencas [Leaves]

Off Period

para Karen y su padre, Juan Rodriguez

I woke up late the next day, baggy eyes, baggy
hearted, weak and got to sit in my room finally—
with the fluorescents off to hide
from them all, hide from the world,
but it didn't last, because esta niña walks in,
don't worry, she's safe still,
she won't get in trouble, she won't get taken
away – she walks in though, asks
mister can I just sit here
for a second,
a minute, a couple of minutes,
a whole fucking 30 minutes
and I never said yes
and she turns around and madre santa,
she starts with this aguacero down her face,
I want to hug this kid and I do,
and I feel this kid, who breaks
into bits of air in the lungs, breaks down
all her words into sobs, into my arms,
into my veins, and there it is
the fear curled in her lips
that perch the words deportation
and and my dad and he signed into
the INS office and and the men
in green, one of them is the same color
as you mister, the same color as me
means he southern Mexican he probably all
Oaxaca or Nayarit or Michoacán, bronze
and he tells my dad – you gonna be a priority
and my dad, he cries, he shakes,
pleads and cresses his hands and he's all
my daughter, she gonna graduación en junio
and Mr. Oaxaca says, then have your ticket
ready for the day after that and I think like a bus
ticket, like a window seat on a plane,
where he has to fight the air pressure,
ears popping and then fight the pressure
and heart strings popping and I don't say shit,

51

I rub her back is what I do—you weren't there
to hear her ribs constrict, to listen to her
teeth clink together, to see her eyes blur
into water pools and all I can think of is
when I was 10 and my old man is thrown
on the ground in Falfurias because
he can't get his green card out fast enough
and I jump on the ground with him, cover
his back with my little frame and I get hit
by a billy club and the guy in green is
the same pendejo, Mr. Oaxaca, I think, and
I don't want her to cry any more
and I don't want me to cry any more
and my shoulder remembers
what residency feels like,
what a split family looks like,
what it looks like to see an oak tree,
the tallest, brownest wood cry, so I want
to tell her she gonna be ok because you are
ok and the bell rings,
she owes me an assignment and she says—
they were gonna deport him now and now
I don't want graduation to come, my parents
can't see me cry and my sister can't see me cry
and I get up and I open the window and
I look at this chrome cloud outside, rain filled,
about ready to burst in the distance and I say,
go there, go hide him there,
til I can think of something, til I can build you
a church to sanctuary his ass in, til I can call
up all the Mexica, til I can find all the obsidian
arrows my elders taught me how to make
for that one good battle, til I can figure out
the work I gotta do to save a Mexican and
she says, mister, we Salvi, from La Unión
and I picture an old girlfriend, in a blue sky
with volcanes and Dios and mamones verdes
plucked and solitude and I ask her—
Can you think of a lie you can tell me
about why you didn't do my reading yesterday?
Mija, tell me anything better than this.

Growl

He is a 9 year old artist—
dirty Filas, ripped jeans.
His home is now the school,
draws forever on the walls.

Creates love notes for chiquitas.
Draws the best sol,
captures largatijos at recess,
king of the columpios.

He won't write in words.
Cries when it's his turn
to read from one book,
rips the pages of a novel.

Trades knuckles with bigger
kids behind the dumpster,
for stealing food from plates.
He is lightweight, the fighter.

He would rather do math.
Figures out his hermanitos'
next four bus stops,
dinner and more markers.

Ignores useless adults.
Tells you straight faced.
His papito huffs paint, says-
papa gives me color headaches.

He just keeps drawing.
Smiles. Says its what feeds him
at night, yet, his stomach,
a skinny long growl at high moon.

When A Student Dies

When you lay there, a brown body floating against
      the edges of a tub, the water warm against
your now cold skin, I hope the last ripples that seep
      into your blood remind you to picture the forest,
the vestments, the wardrobe, the lion's mane,
      and four little white kids you read about days before.
The book, the witch, the rug in my classroom,
      the bookshelf, how check out a book, bookmarks,
the way to turn the page, the way to treat
      a book is the way you hold a child is the way
you should have been held, with your head up,
      your face above the water, not pinned down, no, not
always running from a drunk, run in the fields, hurry,
      defend your life, defend Narnia, live in the back
half of the ropero, escondete hasta que la noche se amaina.
      Imagine warm nights telling Peter and Edmund about
how you beat back a dragon in your real world- off
      the dark streets of Rampart and Renwick. Let
little Lucy smile at you, tell you to sleep in the grass.
      Look up at the stars, eyes closed, your arms floating
by your sides, the edges of grass against your body.
      Listen to the sound of water in the river next to you,
the rain that drops across your face, water all around as you, lay
      there, lay in there, no longer cold, warm, away from harm.
Live with Mr. Tumnus, mijito, live in the pages, live in Narnia,
      where you can hide forever.

**To the Priest Who Told One of My Students
That Holding a Forum on Campus Could Make the Kids Act
Like "the Savage Latinos" He Saw on TV Burning Trump Piñatas**

For Rosemary

When she tells me what you say,
I grip at my chest, drop a few tears.
I think hijo de tu requeté puta madre.
I remember
the four winds wipe away heavy,
that this broad espalda   brings you food,
brings   you the building
you live in.
Me, el mundo named Atlas,   I am
interlaced bone,   the body,
the candles in your cathedral. You, cura—
                    you do not scare me.
You fallible. You petty.
You clutch heartbeats away. You take
meekness and good Catholic Santa Maria,

sharpen a knife with them.   You think
people like me pray like people like you.
You lay miracle hands on ideas
so brilliant you rob them of light. You dark,
your words mince—you want us to
                    remember we are sinners,
you shake the synapse of young minds,
tell them, no, no, be still, a lamb,
awaiting field, wait for the son. But I tell her,
                              I tell them all—
mis hijos, you are the children of the sun.
Our blood is song,   our eyes are
full of letters yet to be written.
Cura, you think we are wild creatures,
you think

we are savages. You think
like every old ass white
man we've had to foot for four hundred

fucking years. No. You flick tongue, preach
pendejadas to young indias, you tell her
that her heart is wrong.
You show her your teeth,
then tell her not to scream.

                           You are alone.

You are the first bestia this child will face—
but I will teach her how to capture you,
yes,   put you in a pen,
line the bottom with scripture,
with your broken homilies,
images of a white Jesucristo.
Make you eat your words, words for days.

Teach her how to cut out your language
filled tripas, how to clean the spineless
white soles you walk on, how to wash
out the fear from   your eyes.

Fill you full of flame and simmer in a pot.
We will feast on you, so, so, slowly.
Watch out—
these savages love the taste of god.

A Saturday Night at the E.R. *(Passin' Me By)*

"Now let me tell you about the feelings I have for you..."
                                        —The Pharcyde

I.

She deserves to breathe.

                                    A single moment
is all she needs.
Some dark, some
quite space, where   closed eyes exist,
recharging   my dear,

                            fulfilling,
                            the heart was
meant to work, my dear.
Breathe in, to do
out, without me
breathe without
me is fine.   My dear,
learn. Breathe again.

II.

Every voice I hear about you, is tender, is comforting, is lost, is bewildered, is
a repeated question, is calm, is unreal, is unwanted, is clueless, is a friend, is a
moment, is spent time to tell you something while you are asleep in the white
room, in a white hospital, in a white linen, in a prayer, in a psalm twenty-three,
in a kiss on the cheek, in a needle replacement, in goes a new IV bag, in a tray of
dry eggs, in a plate of soggy toast, in a week by your side in a grip of your side,
in the pierce of sharp, in between two cold ribs, in a cup for your spit
in when you cough.   No one says a word to me.

                    You do not know me
I am a rock,   unmoving, I suffer with you. I suffer sleepless,
I suffer ache,   I suffer loss, I suffer gray, I suffer you
dirty,   you suffer slow.

III.

I can't help myself,
all I can do is stare,
the hospital gown
you are exposed,
you are seated up,
you arch your back a bit,

to stretch, you have
been in bed for a full day,
your hair hangs
to the right side.   But I know,
I can't daydream,
can't ignore you.

can't want to caress
you like this,   you very well,
not yet, but I will,
once we home,
cover your breasts
with my hands,
change you
out of sweaty sheets,

run you a bath, bathe
you in my palms,
in my breath,
in my dreams,
waiting for the doctor
finish his exam of you.

I can't look away,
you are able
to raise your hands
again,
to take a deep breathe
for the doctor,
and I am angry—

he gets to touch the
middle of your back,
checks your chest
for a murmur, murmurs
you sound better.
You look better,
you look back,
you smile at me,
and I miss you,
my wife, my patient.
Let me get you home.

Requiem for My Mijit@

I am a barrier island, blown
with tepid shores,
with worries that fester up
in slicks of chapopote

at the bottom of feet.
I am an eye sore.
I tremble at crashing waves,
the boom of thunder.

Déjame solo.
Give me a year or more
to lick my wounds,
to clean my shores,

to address the damage.
We lost the inkling of a baby,
the minute I looked at the moon.
I didn't heed the warnings.

I didn't ransack el tendajo
to prep for this devastation.
I was in awe of the swells
on the jetty. I lost my footing,

the expectation of fatherhood—
Instead, the storm sent
us slowly bleeding,
a hurricane inside the womb.

Nothing looks the same.
We waited for it to take its toll.
I am still waiting.
I am a hungry man,

homeless and in need of shelter.
I remember the day
we told my parents
we were having a baby.

They looked at me
said to *wait and see.*
They are not over their loss, either.
I should have an older someone

to collect sand dollars with,
but they were lost
before my birth.
I think, when my father goes fishing,

when my mother looks at the moon,
they are searching for a carita.
They go by night,
tripping around downed palm trees

with a lantern, looking for a lost child.
I should join them,
but I cannot. I am dizzy in sun air.
I bleed salt water onto the road.

I am broken waterlines, uprooted rip-rap.
Forgive me for not wanting
your festivities on my beaches.
I cannot stand the sight—

children, writing their names in gritty me.
It is too soon, this breeze off the pier,
too soon for the seagulls to cackle,
too warped to invite you in.

The Reason We Don't Come Over For Your Daughter's Birthday

is a bittersweet tangerine sized pill I have to swallow every year.
I hope all the beers, the meals I buy you, friend, keep you
from being angry at me. I cannot eat birthday cake.
A crescent moon sliced at my wife's womb the night
I held my goddaughter, and every year when that girl blows
out a candle, we shudder just a tad, a ruffle in our diaphragms—
another year she celebrates without a play pal, that looks like us.

So, How Are You Feeling Today?

When you say the word/pericardium/I think red/I think viscous/I think fragile/I think full/I don't think puncture/I don't see wound/I don't want to know/you can't breathe right/can't catch a gasp/can't sleep laying down/ can't function/You are younger/you take plenty of pills/you have apps on your phone I have to know about/when you fall down/if you fall down/I'm supposed to know/what to do when your fingers turn blue/what to say when they mention renal failure/how to keep a calm demeanor/I tell your parents you are in some ICU/I got the question/are you taking care of her/I just sigh/I just rub your feet/I just wake you/don't yell at me/yell at your puto pericardium/that swells up/a three liter coke bottle full of heavy/fluid/ I don't sleep/you don't sleep/when we do/its two hours/I have bad dreams/ about your heart sack/that wraps you up/clings around your lungs/a knot around your heart/that traipses
around   a   pulse.

You are laying there/wrapped in blankets/wrapped in silver needles/so calm/your face is lying/I watch your ribs rise/bones expand with a jerk/I hear a click/a thud/a white bone is aching/in your side/I should leave/I should get you a pitcher of ice water/fill your cup runneth over/lavish you with unbridled rest/you are in pain there/trying not to make a move/make a sound/make a tear fall/stream down a window pane/looking out into the woods/behind your eyes/in the distance/there are trees/blowing in the gust of wet winds/a few of them/dry and bending/they expand/they click/ twigs inside them break/they grow rigid/they ache/splinters in your heart/ it burns.

It's a waiting game/new tubes of blood/the doctors touch you in places I need candles lit to touch you/soft pillows to caress you/the night moon/showing off your hips/your eyes look at me/in a hunger/hungry for something ripe/ you become restless/want to wrap your legs around my heart/you want to bite into my shoulder blades as if they are mangos/you don't want to be here/see it in your eyes/sunken/dark/you love to hate me/when you are here in the observation room/wires sticking out of your shoulders/out of your breasts/out of your ribs/to get a pulse/to get out of here/you hate me/ for brining you here/to be tested/you teach the pre-med class as they walk in your room/they ask you your history/you show them your heart/in your file/you smile at them/you cry when they leave/you scurry/you fumble around with the tubes/the cords/the drops of tears/the size of stolen bread/ quick/dry them away/they might want to study that too.

Breathe

Lay down in Galveston,
on an August night.

Quietly, so as not to
interrupt the box fan.

Don't fluster the body
into making sweat.

Take a breath in and out.
If the air tastes sweet,

the inhale wasn't ripe
enough. Take longer,

grow it fuller. Drag
the gasp into a draw.

Think of running
in a foot race, foot right,

left foot in, race, trace
the form in, breathe.

Whisper a sweat bead
out. Breathe heavy

with windows open.
Breathe through wrists,

hands, jaw, arms.
Runners don't run with legs.

Breath carries them.
Breath is a breeze

in a metronome, running
with a chest full of salt air

and a beat of sand,
a wave moving though.

#SandySpeaks (For Sandra Bland at the 1st Anniversary of Her Death)

mi abuela dice,
que cuando muere un cuerpo,
they do not end in closed lips.
They breathe last in the breeze,

one that covers you at the panteón,
right when you pass a puño de tierra
al cruzar   el ataúd.
But now, next to this roble,

I wonder   if this summer breeze is
you, Sandra,
                    a constant current that walks
past the road, past the oak, into

the tall grass, into the pines, twined
between the branches of sunlight,
the wave of moths that flutter float
in an evening field. Breath into me,

lady, another song.
Caress my forehead,
comfort my fever with a cool.
                    I want to plant roses for you.

Light a thousand candles, bright enough
to carry me into to the past. I'll take
your place. The news channels will ignore
me. No one covers it when a Mexican hangs.

in Texas. Its enough, I think, to keep you
off that road. Let me be woke. Wake me up
enough to embrace your air. It is the space
where I know you are. You are now

a whirlwind,
a strolling body in every respiro, a gust
that breaks a voice box. Let me shout
your name, a sore throat foot prints in me,

66

one that I will never forget.

Mercy

Immigration officers call
off a massive hunt, state
there are too many
hurricanes in the areas
they want to pick apart.

We go right back to work,
in Houston, ask families
what they need after Harvey.
One lady sits on a chair
outside her place, dips

a piece of mold in her black
coffee. She hands us bricks,
wet ones, says to take them
to help build that new wall,
said they won't even stop

all the rain drops from
crossing over in the night.
A little girl, traces a water
line in crayon in one room,
hasta aquí llego on tippy toes.

Another man, hands us
his dripping eviction
notice, his face is soggy
with fright. He tell us
the cops will be here

soon to kick people into
the water logged street.
He asks us to find the word
mercy in the dictionary,
and rip the damn thing out.

Prayer of a Workhorse

Oh body, do not corner me,
do not grind me into paycheck,

give me a moment of you, body,
a morsel/laugh/eye contact

give me some time to poet,
some time to scribble moon x 100
blue mark black out page stages.

I teach in a brick box. I am metal,
an insurance horse, don't even have

my own dentist/space/shovel.
When I finally die/cry/dream

someone
will have to find me a substitute.

They will be the only one
who thinks of me—

Where did he put all those things?

And I will have to put myself together,
outside the urn, go back to work,

show them where I put those things,
then ask them if they need help.

I carry around a dead voice vase
full of wind. Wander without me,
body. Let me sleep, sleep, sleep in

for the next few days,
pen a particular pillar, mirror it,

wordsmith the shit wick out long
words, out of short words, a short
work week, maybe that is what is

needed. I cannot depend on you
to hear me. You ask too much already.

You so caught up in you, you only
listen to for the word "you". Funny,
I did write them with you in mind.

Dynamite

You see that? Yes,   I am
all the cafecito freckles collected, all
the birthmarks. I am every costa.
                    I am sunlight
held in tan dynamite. When I die,
the world tweets, trends on me,
waits for a coroner's report
and even that shit will be a poem.
250 words will break your heart.
                    When you bury me,
the winds kick up,
so I see all up your skirts, cochinas.
                    When I was born,
all the languages
yelled out

oh Allah, ojala, aw hell nah,

- all the cilantro bowed down
before being picked. All the memes
you see online, are the dreams
I cast when synapses snapped
themself against fiber optic cables
my primos planted in rows,
pum, toma – tu cosecha.
                    I am every grave
found in
Juarez, Sayula, Ayotzinapa,
Queretaro, Mission, El Limón,
La Unión, Villa Grimaldi, Dos Gatos,
Dajabón, Caracas, Jasper, Sugar Land,
the next space, a next space, that next space.
                    When I wash my face
along a Texas coast,
you drink my aqua-bien-fina.
                    When I say
we don't work no more, your kitchen
worker stock plummets, you crumble
with wilted translations,

71

you are at the end of breath.
                              I hold you up.
                              I don't ask you
for money.
                              I vote you off
this puerto, this isla, this canto,
this sueño, this trago, this alma.
I might not let you back in.
Go ahead, get on
the other side of that wall –

you want to live without me
so much, vamos a ver cómo te va.

Part IV—Maguey [Body]

A Mujercita's Profile Drawing at the East End Studio Gallery, "Transition"

You keep your eyes shut.   Blanquita skin
shines bright. A chin turn to the left. You are quiet,

you bury yourself in this rostro. Pose a bit longer.
A right shoulder up, the angle takes the whole space,

a good eight and a half by eleven. Perch out
that ruca neck tattoo. Everybody can see you, toda

chingona. Do you wonder if people talk about you?
You used to people staring at you outside of this drawing?

You bite your bottom lip a bit,   trembling in red,
you sink in this moment, a comfort. You remember,

tu madre don't fucking like the use of needles   in you,
in your skin. The silver ones scar, bruise you, in jeringa sweats—

the ones dripping the word *mom*, a bundle in teal colored roses
you suffered. You always close your eyes. There are whispers,

talk, about the delicate petals on your clavicle. You always
arch your back, reeling in a glass cylinder, that tinta,   toxicity

of an old school chola. You do this drawing a favor. You hate
photos, but this, this isn't so quick.

This is so good, it can take a bit.
You take a breath away, draw in eyes close,   thinking,

the last time you see the house, mother, or pretty on the wall,
brilliant sparks, a billion specks trace around you, in your head.

You clean up nice, yo. You remember her embrace.
Fingers race to run around the base of your neck, following

las rosas, the lines of your cheek bones, your ears.
The colors of the teal, the center of the drawing,   the roses

makes gente want to touch you for real.   Supple, deep,
fleshy roses, her arms bundle around you. They don't exist

in teal. Say her name. Her name in your skin makes you miss her.
Everybody wants to know your name. You do not hesitate
outside of this frame. You own every pose. You won't tell
anyone about mom, about you. You don't talk to her. But here,

no one can tell that. Here, you are sure. Here don't let tremble in,
against this canvas. You brush away your pain, put up your hair,

you look beautiful, that way.
                                                  Look that way.

Flight (On June Jordan's "Free Flight")

There is never enough travel to keep you
home,
a back pack, ready,
rolled up maps, socks, undies,
a vile of holy water, sage in a bag
                    for the spirits that travel,
                              that haunt
you too, carry all the ghosts on shoulders, in that bag
filled, crammed   with passport forms,
thumb print scans ,   a room with your shit
laid out on a table, rummage this again,
Mr. TSA Agent, yes, sir,
                  no, sir,   why the gloves?
That's not a liquid,
                it's a sensitive skin,
teal colored   Gillette eight ounce gel,
that's not a weapon,
        it's a butter knife
for the bread and the decadent, yes,
slick Nutella.   Ask him for that.
        You have not   eaten.
                    The line is longer
when you get out,
        finally,
you are not a terrorist,   just checking,
upload all the photos,   the blog post,
photo-bomb   the shit out of Westminster,
pay three times to get   in the Tate Modern,
explode your eyes at the Tate Modern,
over   and over   and over,
        over a pint of Carling
with a pretty Irish girl,
        walk her to her place
near Chairing Cross, cross the street,   in the puddles,
in the sprinkle, in the gray,   change the gray
to night, dejadaté un momentito en Russell Square—
change clothes, a black Mossimo V-neck
for a heavy polo, fifty percent cotton,
fifty percent, hot,   sweaty,

                    walk, you,   you fat ass, walk,
walk, then pack again,   pay the fare, the transfer,
the taxi, to
            get you to Stansted,
the Costa coffee with soy one percent milk,
with a baguette and gouda cheese and a half a Roma tomato,
for a bit,   pop in the plane,   a fifty dollar flight
for a twenty pound note,
                            fiberglass bus seat
on a plane- no safety instructions,
            no upright tray table,
just buckle your ass in
            or you will slide down the tarmac
in Madrid
            Chicago
                    Miami
as soon as you land.   Throw out all the clothes
        you put in the bag,   dip them in Lysol,
dip them in honey,   dip them in boiling water,
get the scent   of exploration   off of them,
get off,
        come on,   you only have another twenty
                            minutes,
before she has to leave for her flight,
remember she needs you around
                    before you
have to leave for Austin
                Anaheim,
por el amor de Dios,
hurry up and see   you both,   alone,   a sliver of a minute,
don't talk   too much,   take the sad look

                            out of your pupil,
you didn't have to   leave   for so   long,
between the rush of conversation-
did you feed the dog
                    yes
walk the dog
                    aw fuck
remember to call me
                    bought you a snow globe in July
Check the dinner,

                    78

                    eat the dinner,
fix the breakfast,
        boil the eggs,
                pay a bill   late
        she says she is

                                late,
try to talk about it when you drop her   off
for her next flight   hug right,
plan for this   new thing,   get all tired   at home,
                rock me to sleep,
                        sleep,

                                        sleep,
                        dream,

get up, take a leak,
take a shower, call to say,   say goodbye,
                forget   to say goodbye.
Then, forget   the names   of the days of the week
or that time changes
or that you forgot to,   remember to check
back with her   doctor, waiting on the line,
another moment   stuck in a line,
a trip,
        what a trip,
                another minute   to see that
no one in this place   is going exactly   where you are.
Stand still, would you?

Photograph of "Woman on Street—Flower Leis"

The title of the photo is wrong.
You are not on the street—you are hovering.
Your feet crossed, goddess,
barefoot, tender feet, no ankles here,
hiding under a woven, wool, waist-wide falda,

trim in red and you wear a white blusa,
green vines array flowers that fleck and burst in
purple down your neck, a thick neck,
a worker's neck, a young lover's neck,
and around this, una cadena de caléndulas,

    rojo, amarillo, rojo, amarillo, rojo, rojo, amarillo, nuca, y el patron sigue.

Una corona, mi reina, te alumbra el rosto,
estas caléndulas sirven, ángel con tu aureola,
ángel con tus brazos medios extendidos a los lados,
lista para dicha palabra, holding a lei in each hand,

    red, yellow, red, yellow, red, red, yellow, finger tips, the pattern continues.

You sit in a makeshift thrown, in front of a fountain,
the two stone men behind you carved into the wall,
one to each side, always genuflect, pay respects, still,
their large hands, the size of yours, cover their faces
with water. You perch, bird of the day. You reign,
diosa. Matlalcueye, you don't smile, you don't

move, detienes tu pecho, above the water
in the fountain pool behind you. Turn your body
around, dip your feet in the cool of the water, in
the wet of the stone, in the middle of your day,
y luego bendiga todo con una mirada de tus ojos.

A Human Rights Worker Tells Me About the Cuarenta y tres

"Vivos se los llevaron, vivos los queremos"
—*rally cry for the 43 missing Nornalistas*

a voice on the other end of a phone ring,
a whisper, checks the door, a look through the blinds,
an ok, no hay nadie aquí—
a breath, a flood of words that reverses blood flow,
the voice on the other end, he, could not let
his tongue slow down, could not let the air
come out of his lungs without llanto
filling the line, the whole room, the whole one
thousand, one hundred and thirty four miles between
there and here—the voice trembles—
there are over one hundred students
there, in the town square, the ones
who come from the mountains – he says, the ones
who want to go back to their homes,
teach Mixtecos how to come out from mountains.
One of them, he's been found, in the moon
light, in the middle of the street, his hands,
dirty from the blood in the puddles, and his face,
not fit for the classroom he wants to teach in,
but a face, a something Posada would have drawn,
a round, pink set of bones, not the skin, not the lips,
but the white cheek, the jaw, the brow exposed
to the evening breeze. This body has been drug
by a car – he says, the police didn't help this
soon to be teacher, no, they let him fall in the mud.
Let the face melt away along the brick road. This body,
this boy isn't the only fracaso. He's not the only one
who's missing. The voice on the phone—help me,
gasps for air –help me find the foot prints, the rumors,
los ojos, the bus tickets, los escapularios, the wallets,
las fotos, the cell phones, las huellas, the watches,
la voz juvenil, the shoes, las venas, the breast plates,
el aliento of forty-two more just like him. Help me,
he whispers,
see if we can find their faces in la selva,
help me see if we can find them

in the mouth of mayor's wife, tan golosa,
can't lick her fingers fast enough, she can't
even eat all the names at once, without taking
a moment to look around. She doesn't want to be
seen, esa dama, eating the fruit, la cosecha—Ayotzinapa.
But she will eat nonetheless, binge on silent bodies,
until her teeth hide all the limbs, leave only bones,
charred speeches, decay and a rot from such young meat.

A Dancer Tells Me About the Cuarenta y Tres
(Para Christian Alfonso Rodriguez Telumbre)

> *Y en los suspiros decia el que la seca la llena*
> *—Las Amarillas, Arturo Villela Hernández*

It is a hot night when I take the stage, I know these steps,
una lucha para mi, a flutter in the lights, a flock of birds in
my head, a rhythm I can not step away from. My home,
my Guerrero, suffers a loss, an absence, cuarenta y tres are

missed. When I look up at the sky – could not see los pajaros
cadernales, I race to put on my dance shoes, to hug
my children, to count the heads in my own classroom,
race to say the names of forty three sons, gone somewhere,

engrave them on my dance shoe tacones. I want a saneamiento,
dress up in a huipil, a yellow skirt, a field of yellow flowers
in my hair. I heard el gavilán say "A mi hijo, le gusta bailar
ballet folklórico", it echoes desde la costa de mi Acapulco,

across the mountains in Ayotzinapa, up this border. I let
the pañuelo flicker around the air, the bird that flows,
buscando respuesta, un nido, un respiro.
He came to find his son, to ask for help, to dance a cumbia

with me, to watch us, came to watch me dance Las Amarillas,
and every step was a pounding fight with shadows, the longest
I have ever danced. I can't watch the rostros in the crowd,
feel the tears well up on my face, I keep the beat, close

my eyes every few breaths, look around, think I see el pico
pico, a young normalista, bring his own paliacate and share
a dance with me. It is an ofrenda, una llamada, an echo,
a marcha, a fogata, a fight, a linterna, a flare, a beckoning,
a rezo, a pause, un movimiento led with a simple handkerchief.

I make this gavilán, Clemente, cry tonight, hypnotize him

with a bandada that glows, make his heart swell, remind
him of a brilliant picture, a tarima and his son, caught up

in a dance, watch his lips as he mentions his son,
all our sons will dance once more.

Photograph of "Woman in Red Dress, Sunflowers, Sitting With Blanket"

Óigame, doña, ¿y esos mirasoles? ¿a cuanto los vende? Ándele, véndeme las
¿no? Y la cobija también, que las líneas en negro y blanco remind me of a tent
entrance to a circus at the edge of a field, a field in Tlajomulco, so straight, so
propped up, parece capa, eres majestad con esa capa, at the edge of you y los
mirasoles, they grow out of you right now, you grow out of the wall, you grow
into the sky, your trenzas are long stem stocks tied in bright yellow orange,
you grow into the clouds, the white ones that sit next to you, your hair Doña,
enrollado en rayos de sol, amarillo profundo, véndeme su pelo, los rayos,
ándele, doña, no sea mala, véndemelas ¿no? No, no sus ojos, ni su respiro,
pero las flores, I am sorry, I should have complemented you on your purple,
tu rosada, tu morada, your pink vestido, lleno de lunares, la cobija lleno de
rayas en los rayos del sol, el sol, el sol que la cubre en un fulgor, que la cubre,
que el sol extiende su boca y bese su piel, un beso en su frente, que brille, que
brille, que brille. Perdón, doña, véndeme su tiempo, su silencio, su espacio en la
pared, sus pies que no puedo ver, su manos que son mirasoles, hecho de nubes,
hecho de rostro, hecho de paz, de paz, de paz, mejor, la dejo doña, la dejo, la
dejo solita,
mirasol, en paz.

An Only Child

is a raindrop   one that travels
between the ridges of tree bark.
He is fake menopause. She is
unwanted at first. He is born
an accident.

She is on a time clock
from her first breath. He accepts
being   forgotten on his birthday.

An only child

carries their parents   once
they pass away. She asks
too many   questions.
He is always and never alone.   She
doesn't know the world   without

daydreaming. He learns
to look for voices instead of people.
She builds her own brothers and sisters.
He knows how to live and die
     alone before anyone else.

An only child

is a final stock bond blooming
DNA in an IVF hook up.   He
contemplates fucking up
       his pull out game. She wonders if
the family tree stops at her.

He adapts to scenes—a bruto
transformer at the [insert name of event or venue].
She counts trust as a blade of war.

An only child

is a fighting leon/a surrounded

86

by hyenas.   He is a barbaro
amongst a room full of laughs. She is most
confortable/uncomfortable with no one else.
And when
one only child meets another for
the first time,
     they move with caution,   slowly
reading   the eyes,
 watching   the hands   to see
if they might have been some related
seeds scattered by a storm or
                  a strong wind.

Un soñador al momento que le dicen que no

for all the inmigrantes, adelante

Es un roble en calles inundadas,
tiene ideas cubiertas en llamas,
es luz, es raíz, es el rayo a lo oscuro
se vista de catrín y dama,
soldado de la inteligencia,
cura de ignorancia,
y platica,
y platica
y planifica,
convierte pierda y palabra
mala a trozos de oro para su nido
—vive en lucha,
canta de paz,
sus pensamientos son
las estrellas de noche,
nubes expandidas al día,
es caballero en armadura,
armadura ya hecho
de bendiciones y tierra,
vive con sus manos llenas
de ofrendas, de memoria
su corazón es jarro,
moldeado por sus padres,
sus huesos son fierro
a los golpes, sus golpes
son semillas plantadas
por donde camina,
su camino es largo,
su paso es ancho,
su respiro—el sonido de alas,
un millón de alas en el viento,
sus ojos contienen la corona
del sol
el soñador vive
cuando sigue,
cuando sigue,
cuando brille

Astra (Pantoum en el cielo)

Se encontraba reparando un vehículo
Chevrolet Astra, de modelo reciente,
al parecer de su propiedad, cuando
fue atacado por sus victimarios. Respira.

Era un Chevrolet Astra, recientemente pintado
azul marino, con una raya amarilla por arriba.
Fue atacado por sus victimarios en la luz
del día. Su mujer se arrimo a su cuerpo después.

El cielo, azul marino, con una raya amarilla,
llovió en el medio día, un relámpago entregado,
cuando cayo, nadie mas se arrimo a su cuerpo.
Sintió el treno en el aire, las gotas de lluvia

en el medio día, vio un relámpago entregado,
un rayo lo tocó, le tronó su pecho.
Sintió el treno en el aire, las gotas de sangre.
En los últimos momentos de su vida,

un rayo lo tocó, una bala le tronó su pecho.
Era el tiempo de las aguas en Zapopan
en los últimos momentos de su vida.
Las tormentas le daban taquicardia.

Era el tiempo de las aguas en Zapopan
cuando conoció a su amante. Respiró.
Cada noche con ella le daba taquicardia.
Quería terminar con su Chevrolet Astra.

cuando conoció a sus amante, sonrío.
Se entrego a los últimos arreglos, apurado,
quería terminar con su Chevrolet Astra,
venderlo, zafarse del mal gasto, comprometerse.

Se entrego a los últimos arreglos, una boda,
con la hija de la vecina, su amante. Vio su vida,
lo vendió, se zafo del mal gasto, se comprometió.
Al tomar sus últimos respiros de un aire dulce,

La hija de la vecina, su amante, corrió a ver su vida,
Tuvo treinta y dos años de edad, al salir de su casa
Al tomar sus últimos respiros de un aire dulce,
se entrego a las ultimas memorias, la voz de su amor.

Tuvo treinta y dos años de edad, al salir de su casa,
no temo ver su sangre el momento que llego la bala.
Se entrego a las ultimas memorias, la voz de su amor,
cuando se encontraba reparando su vehículo. El Astra.

List of Locations Where Mexicans Have Been Denied Service
(Found Poem)

—From the Alfonso S. Perales Papers, Approx. 1940's

SAN ANGELO, TEXAS.

Curry Drug Store,
Texas Grill,
N. Chadbourne St.,
owner, George Wylie,   Se niega servicio a mexicanos.

Red Top Inn,
1320 N. Chadbourne St.
owner, Ed Motl,   Se niega servicio a mexicanos.

ROTAN, TEXAS.

City Barbershop,
Vittitow Barber Shop,
Alton Parker Barber Shop,   Todas estas barberías
                                 negaron servicio   al Sargento
                                 Alejandro Martínez,   al Paracaidista
                                 Frank Vélez;   al soldado
                                 Guillermo González,   y a cincuenta
                                 soldados México-Americanos más.

BLUNTZER, TEXAS.
                                 Los niños
                                 mexicanos están   separados
de los niños anglo-americanos
en las escuelas elementales.
El mejor edificio
lo usan los anglo-americanos   mientras
                                 que los niños mexicanos se educan
                                 en un jacal   destartalado.

MIDLAND, TEXAS.

                                 Los mexicanos son segregados
                                 y se les obligue a que usen

un balcón
para Negros

en la sección reservada
en los teatros
Yucca, Ritz y Rex.

A los mexicanos,
se les niega el servicio en los restaurante

En el Ritz Café
hay un rótulo que dice:
[AQUI NO SE ADMITE

MEXICANOS].
[AQUI NO SE ADMITE MEXICANOS

CORPUS CHRISTI, TEXAS.

A un Conceller del Consulado de Méxic
se le cobró diez centavos
que valía solamente cinco,

por una soda
en el "Drive-In Stand."

Cuando preguntó porqué
se le cobraba esa cantidad,
se le contesto
que porque era   mexicano.

Photograph of "Woman on Street – Blue Scarf, Red Dress"

"Dona Maria como vai você ?"

—*Traditional Capoeira Song*

You are the third woman I find
no shoes,   with no home,
in bright colors,   in closed eyes.

you are waiting for a fight,   the hate,
the waiting for someone   to come
                              back.
If I didn't know any   better,
I'd say you've been waiting   a bit

"said he'd be back in three days,
he left me here on these sharp rocks,
        took my shoes so I can't leave,
don't want to slice each sole down to the muscle"

        I want to say a prayer with you,
but you are not that María, you tell me
it would be a waste   *of your time,*
a waste of your day,   *a waste of a virgen,*

maybe you should stand up
 in that red skirt, in that blue reboso,
        and march around,
maybe go collect   that last conversation,

the set of words you   have pursed
in your lips, in an image   in your head,
I know you are a bit punchy.
             I am sorry
to take your picture,   but I want to take you
                 with me,

you don't want to be left here,
you hate him, that someone,
       want to grind him with your teeth.

I won't tell anyone   if you don't believe
                                    in a god.
Cut him in his side,   make him
wish he never crossed you.

Violent Before the Moon (Para Huitzilopochtli)

Inside mi madre, I kept blades in my arms
my legs bent, escondí ojos en mis manos.
I imagined what I would say

what the air felt like. I dreamt people wanted
to touch the sun but I let the stain of foul
words press against my ears.

Inside I wanted el toque de luz. She let me
know what they said about her, lo que
pensaban de mí, of how quickly I had grown

in her belly, I wrestled within every
floating thought. Esperé tenso, hasta que mi
madre me dejó salir, let me finally face

the audience, with eyes ready to carve me. But
I remembered—mother
said something in a nectar voice—

Huitz, querido mijito, vístete, hold tight to me,
I need you to be ready. Ponte tu mejor traje.

I remembered my sister spat obscenities,
lashing out, how mother was too old to have
four hundred and two mouths to feed.

She called my mother a puta, muchacha que ni
un dedo para apuntar a la tierra, she, who fooled
around with warriors en el templo, she laughed

at her own magic tricks. She killed mother.
There was no light left in madre, just the blades
I unfurled in my arms. My legs pounced

at my sister, cutting her, threw her beautiful face
her, the moon – then turned to my brothers,
sisters, who looked so vast, made them look

at our mother. Rindieron culto a ella con
un centelleo, con luminiscencia. I made
them the stars. I hid my eyes in the end,

felt the air on my face. I dreamt people
who touched the sun, now the moon, every night.

Angustia vs. Silence

I cannot help you.   When you cry
you hide inside a cave,   under the dark
a rock, a mushroom,   you can't even speak
won't budge,   won't share grief
someone told you that a woman   that cries
is weak or that   emotion is a hot blanket
that makes everyone   uncomfortable and
I know, at night,   when we sleep, I
jerk and moan, you   wince and I haven't
even touched you, it is   all the corked up tears
your eye ducts have   recorded all the falls
a quite birthday party   every year and
only five people show up.   I won't let you in.
Its my fucking house.   I am Ponce de Leon
and I claim you, my island,   in the name of grief.
Pop you, you big red balloon   I think
flinch will make you shudder.   One day all that energy
will flow right out of you,   wildly, will burst. A molotov
brakes against some wall   up in my insides. I want
you to stop running away   from you, end up in a circle,
out of breathe, lost so   just sit with me. Let me touch
those nerves, untangle   the veins coiled around your heart,
the damn things ache so much.   I can see it in your silence.
You sit there doing nothing.   You wear sulk until it stinks.
I do not think I can help.   You don't recognize these
gestures, plates brake on   walls, a punch at the ribs,
a pot of scalding water   across my arms, a hand between
the frame and its door,   a frozen beer hurts only a few
minutes , throb, hurts   cracks in a skull. I know these things.
it is the home of impatience   you live in. I bounce around
on the inside, grow thick skin,   can see fists
flinging at me, a whirl of gran maul   seizure strikes
at my back, a trail of belt buckles   latches on to my lips,
and I bleed. I know when hate   decides where he stands,
leans, in the door. Drunk. Lost   in a moment. Get lost with me,
just like that. Make it intimate.   Throw a few things,
join this ruckus, the one time,   I am used to. Let your body
flex a few screams, don't worry,   I can take the hits.
At least I know you, at the end of it all   you will sleep.

An Only Child (A Final Note)

I have always hid in a comic book.
Most of these heroes, these villains
grew up as an only child.

I am Kyle Rayner's medio hermano

Mil Gracias

Primeramente, para mi wifey, Jasminne Mendez, y mi hija, Luz Maria—who provide me with the love, the energy, el hogar and the words I need to keep this craft alive. Amo, thank you for being there, sitting with me as I sat with my self–doubt. Thank you for believing in me, even when I forgot to. You are my spirit. You are my compass. Luz Maria, mi reina, you are less than a year old as this book sees print. One day when you are old enough, I hope you get to know me a little bit better. Eres mi todo.

Para mis padres, Pedro and Eusebia Mendez, de quien aprendí la definición de familia, fe, amor y humildad. You are my rock; you are my home. Thank you for being who you are. Through my lips, you always speak. Los quiero con todo corazón.

To Tony Diaz, the crew of Nuestra Palabra (Alvaro, Icess, both Carolinas, Russell, Radames, Bryan, Liana, Chuy, Laura and Angie) and all the Librotraficantes for giving me a space to write, a space to create, a foundation in words and the tools to make a change in the world I live in. You opened doors to the Latino literary world that have transformed my life. I can only hope to repay you with good deeds and opening that same door for future writers.

To all the CantoMundistas past, present and future, you are always familia. Thank you for sharing your words, your world and your thoughts with me. I am a better writer for having spent time with you. Please know, I am here to support what you do – unidos siempre. A major Shout Out to Yesenia Montilla, Laurie Ann Guerrero, Peggy Robles - Alvarado, Urayoan Noel, Rosebud Ben-Oni, Jose Araguz, Malcolm Friend, Christian Olivares, Noel Quiñones, Sheila Maldonado, Denice Frohman, Raina Leon, Vanessa Angélica Villarreal, Javier Zamora, Anthony Cody, Marcelo Hernandez Castillo, Juan Morales, Octavio Quintanilla, Cassandra Lopez and Eduardo Gabrieloff – thank you for always being there, familia.

To the Texas Gulf Coast poetry/arts scene, especially Jonathan Moody, Stephen Gros, Deniz Lopez, Natasha Carrisoza, Deborah Mouton, Ching –In Chen, Robin Davidson, Daniel Peña, Outspoken Bean, thefluentone, Marcel Murphy, Erika Jo Brown, BJ Love, Chris Wise, Lizbeth Ortiz, Trevor and Kayla Baffone, Hugo Rodriguez, Marlon Lizama, the poets of the Word Around Town Poetry Tour, my RGV family—Edward Vidaurre, Emmy Perez, Rodney Gomez, Amalia Ortiz, Inprint (Rich Levy, Krupa

Parikh, Kristen, Ann, Marilyn), Mauricio Campos, the Brazilian Arts Foundation, Senzala (Alvin Brown), Bombril (Damon Bowen) and Tony Parana—for your support, your encouragement and your passion. I am the writer I am because of you. To the younger poets & writers, Ayokunle, Josh, Cristina, Zach, Torrina, Xach, Ryan and many others—I am a sharper writer because of you.

To the students, faculty and staff of the University of Texas @ El Paso's MFA ONLINE Creative Writing Program, especially Sasha Pimentel, Tim Z. Hernandez, Daniel Chacon, Lex Williford, Jeff Serkin and Jose de Pierola, thank you for your encouragement, your honesty, your embrace of this writer. I can honestly say, I am grateful you took a chance on me and have nothing but the utmost respect for you and this program. I talk to fellow poets about their MFA experiences, and I am proud to say, I went with a damn fine program that cares for its writers. I will always sing your praises.

To my crew—from Galveston to UST and beyond—Barbara, Dan, Marina, Yolanda, Joe, Angie, Aaron, Ivy, Georgette, Jon, Emily, James, Alex. Mi gente, my head and my heart. Thank you for making sure I didn't die along the way. You've seen me at my worst, thank you for hanging around for my best.

To Aquarius Press/ Willow Books—Heather and Randall and everybody else, thank you for having faith in my work. Thank you for taking care of this writer and giving these poems a home. You've made this one of the best experiences ever, a dream I am still dreaming.

To all the literary organizers and open-mic hosts and all the grass roots arts organizations—I see you. I thank you for the work you do. You tow the line that makes this art form fire. The majority of the poems here were written with you in mind. You have a special place in my heart.

And to you the reader, mil gracias for taking a chance on this work.

About the Poet

Originally from Galveston, TX, Mendez (Writer//Educator//Activist) works with Nuestra Palabra: Latino Writers Having Their Say, Brazilian Arts Foundation and other organizations to promote poetry events, advocate for literacy/literature and organize creative writing workshops that are open to the public. He is the founder of Tintero Projects and works with emerging Latinx writers and other writers of color within the Texas Gulf Coast Region. Lupe co-hosts *INKWELL*, a collaborative podcast on regional, national and international Latinx writers and other writers of color. Mendez is a CantoMundo Fellow, a Macondo Fellow and an Emerging Poet Incubator Fellow.

Mendez has nearly 20 years of experience as a performance poet, having opened up for such notable writers as Dagoberto Gilb, Esmeralda Santiago and the late Raul Salinas. He has shared his poetry across the country in places such as the Holocaust Museum Houston, the Jung Center, MECA (Houston), the Mission Cultural Center For Latino Arts (San Francisco), the National Hispanic Cultural Center (Albuquerque) and the Mexican American Cultural Center (Austin). A keynote speaker/poetry performer across Texas, Mendez hosts writing workshops across the country, most recently as a teaching artist for the Poetry Foundation's Teacher Poetry Summits.

Mendez is an internationally published writer with prose work in *Latino Rebels, Houston Free Press, the Kenyon Review* and Norton's *Sudden Fiction Latino: Short-Short Stories From The United States and Latin America, Flash* (University of Chester, England), and poetry in *The Bayou Review* (University of Houston-Downtown), *Huizache, Luna Luna Magazine, Pilgrimage, Texas Review, Bordersenses, HeART Journal Online, Glass Poetry Journal, Tinderbox Poetry Journal, Voluable* and *Gulf Coast Journal,* among others.

Mendez has been honored as one of Houston Press' "Creative 100s" and was also awarded a Downs Intellectual Freedom Award for the defense of Mexican American Studies and literature across the Southwest United States. Mendez's work reflects his roots in Texas and the Mexican state of Jalisco. Mendez is the son of an undocumented Mexicano and a Southern Tejana and his work remarks on issues from the political to the emotional in a way that intends to connect with both the novice reader to the pro poetic writer.

Printed in the USA
CPSIA information can be obtained
at www.ICGtesting.com
LVHW102334210823
755812LV00005B/188